Using Literature To Learn About The First Americans

A Thematic Approach To Cultural Awareness

by Judith Cochran

Incentive Publications, Inc.
Nashville, Tennessee

Illustrated by L. K. Hill
Cover by Susan Eaddy
Edited by Jan Keeling

ISBN 0-86530-262-6

Table of Contents

Student Activity Pages

PREFACE

This ready-to-use thematic unit provides everything an educator needs to teach a fully integrated two-week-long course of study of Native Americans, including lesson plans, teacher's guide, and reproducible student worksheets. Many school systems now base their curricula on broad themes and student outcomes, a practice which allows teachers a great deal of flexibility when selecting units. Instead of textbooks, the teaching books of choice are literature books and information books. The topics are broad so that children will learn *all* of the basics—in this book there are specific activities in every subject, including Reading, Writing, Math, Science, Social Studies, and Art. All of the work of pulling together information and legend theory into an integrated whole has been done for you.

This study of Native Americans need not be presented in strict accordance with the outlined two-week schedule. There are many ways to use this book! The unit is so packed with activities and information, it can easily be extended to fit a schedule longer than two weeks. Some educators prefer to spend at least two days on a literature book (even a short primary-level book). You may include information books with your literature lessons so that children may do research, writing, and presentations along with their activities. *Using Literature To Learn About The First Americans* is also an invaluable resource for a traditional textbook-driven classroom, as it enriches, reinforces skills, educates, and provides across-the-curriculum activities and opportunities for further study and growth.

Each lesson is detailed in the teacher's guide pages (11–50) with concepts broken down into an easy-to-follow format. Student activity pages (51–77) are easy to understand and ready to use as reproducible blackline masters. For further study, additional books and projects are suggested (78–79).

The six groups of Native Americans presented in this book are:

- Southwest (Navaho)
- Plains (Comanche/Cheyenne)
- Southeast (Cherokee)
- Algonquin (Ojibwa)
- Northwest (Tlingit)
- Eskimo (Inuit)

The books you will need for this unit are:

Southwest

Turquoise Boy, by Terri Cohlene. New Jersey: Watermill Press, 1990.

When Clay Sings, by Byrd Baylor. New York: Aladdin Books, 1972.

Plains

The Legend of the Bluebonnet, by Tomie dePaola. New York: G.P. Putnam's Sons, 1983.

The Girl Who Loved Wild Horses, by Paul Goble. New York: Aladdin Books, 1978.

Southeast

Dancing Drum, by Terri Cohlene. New Jersey: Watermill Press, 1990.

Algonquin

The Rough-Face Girl, by Rafe Martin. New York: G.P. Putnam's Sons, 1992.

The Star Maiden, by Barbara Juster Esbensen. Boston: Little, Brown and Co., 1988.

Northwest

How Raven Brought Light to People, by Ann Dixon. New York: Margaret K. McElderry Books, 1992.

Eskimo

Song of Sedna, by Robert San Souci. New York: Doubleday, 1981.

Ecology of Native Americans

Brother Eagle, Sister Sky, by Susan Jeffers. New York: Dial Books, 1991.

Special materials required for various activities are:

- Ears of multicolored Indian corn (MATH: pg. 12)
- Beans and tortillas, etc. (SOC. STUDIES: pg. 17)
- Large paper bags (ART: pg. 30)
- Ingredients for Corn Meal Pancakes & Maple Syrup (SOC. STUDIES: pg. 33)
- Salad macaroni and food coloring (ART: pg. 34)
- Sugar cubes, margarine tubs for igloo model (ACT. CHOICES: pg. 48)
- Assorted cans, bottles w/plastic lids, and beans (ACT. CHOICES: pg. 49)
- Plastic drinking straws, string, medium-sized paper bags, paper plates for various projects

Sending this list home to parents as a "wish list" can be helpful.

READY-TO-USE THEMATIC UNIT OUTLINE (WEEK ONE)

MONDAY	TUESDAY	WEDNESDAY	THURSDAY	FRIDAY
Southwest Indians	Southwest Indians	Plains Indians	Plains Indians	Southeast Indians
READ ALOUD: Turquoise Boy (Cohlene) Teacher Page 11	**READ ALOUD:** When Clay Sings (Baylor) Teacher Page 15	**READ ALOUD:** The Legend of the Blue-bonnet (de Paola) Teacher Page 19	**READ ALOUD:** The Girl Who Loved Wild Horses (Goble) Teacher Page 23	**READ ALOUD:** Dancing Drum (Cohlene) Teacher Page 27
WRITING: Chart Story: The Navaho Indians Teacher Page 11	**WRITING:** Descriptive Writing: Draw/Write Descriptions of Clay Bowl Teacher Page 15 Student Page 56	**WRITING:** Indian Names Teacher Page 19	**WRITING:** Character Analysis: Explain Why Girl Wants to Live With Horses Teacher Page 23	**WRITING:** Predicting Outcomes: What If The Sun Didn't Shine? Teacher Page 27
READING EXPERIENCE: If I Were Navaho Teacher Page 11 Student Page 51	**READING EXPERIENCE:** Comprehension: Draw Clay Bowl From Written Description Teacher Page 16 Student Page 56	**READING EXPERIENCE:** Sign Language Story Teacher Page 19	**READING EXPERIENCE:** Summarizing/ Finger Puppets Teacher Page 24 Student Page 61	**READING EXPERIENCE:** Summarizing in Written Form Teacher Page 28 Student Page 64
MATH: Estimating Teacher Page 12 Student Page 52	**MATH:** Symmetry Teacher Page 16 Student Page 57	**MATH:** Fractions Teacher Page 20 Student Page 59	**MATH:** Geometric Shapes/ Designs Teacher Page 24 Student Page 62	**ACTIVITY CHOICES:** Paper Plate Masks Teacher Page 28 Act Out Indian Stories Teacher Page 29 Travois Model Teacher Page 29
SCIENCE: Corn Cycle Teacher Page 13 Student Page 53	**SCIENCE:** Triarama: Animals of the Desert Teacher Page 17 Student Page 58	**SCIENCE:** The Rain Cycle Teacher Page 21 Student Page 60	**SCIENCE:** Categorize Plains Animals Teacher Page 25 Student Page 63	**SOCIAL STUDIES:** Map, Cherokee History Teacher Page 30 Student Pages 54, 65
SOCIAL STUDIES: Map, Navaho Life Teacher Page 13 Student Pages 54, 55	**SOCIAL STUDIES:** Beans and Tortillas Teacher Page 17	**SOCIAL STUDIES:** Map Teacher Page 21 Student Page 54	**SOCIAL STUDIES:** Indian Poster Teacher Page 25	**ART:** Buckskin Vest Teacher Page 30
ART: Weaving Teacher Page 14	**ART:** Clay Pot Teacher Page 18	**ART:** Paper Plate Shields Teacher Page 22	**ART:** Tepee Model Teacher Page 26	

9

READY-TO-USE THEMATIC UNIT OUTLINE (WEEK TWO)

	MONDAY	TUESDAY	WEDNESDAY	THURSDAY	FRIDAY
	Algonquin (Northeast) Indians	Algonquin (Northeast) Indians	Northwest Indians	Eskimo	Ecology of Native Americans
READ ALOUD:	*The Rough-Face Girl* (Martin) Teacher Page 31	*The Star Maiden* (Esbensen) Teacher Page 35	*How Raven Brought Light to People* (Dixon) Teacher Page 39	*Song of Sedna* (San Souci) Teacher Page 43	*Brother Eagle, Sister Sky* (Jeffers) Teacher Page 47
WRITING:	Similarities/Differences of Story to Cinderella Teacher Page 31	What Form Would You Take If You Were Star Maiden? Teacher Page 35	Writing From Fact About Northwest Indians Teacher Page 39	What Did You Think Happened After the End of the Story? Teacher Page 43	Write Letter to Chief Seattle Teacher Page 47
READING EXPERIENCE:	Story Frame: Characters, Problem, Solution Teacher Page 31 Student Page 66	Foldbook: Beginning/Middle/End of Story Teacher Page 35 Student Page 69	Predicting Outcomes: How Would Life Be Different Without The Sun? Teacher Page 39	Sequencing Events of Story Teacher Page 43 Student Page 75	**ACTIVITY CHOICES:** Sugar Cube Igloo Teacher Page 48 Cook Indian Pudding Teacher Page 49 Drums/Rattles/Dances/Chants Teacher Page 49
MATH:	Patterning Teacher Page 32 Student Page 67	Moccasin Measuring Teacher Page 36 Student Page 70	Following Directions: Make One of Raven's Boxes Teacher Page 40 Student Page 73	Understanding Temperature Teacher Page 44 Student Page 76	
SCIENCE:	Uses of Birch Bark Teacher Page 32 Student Page 68	Parts of a Flower Teacher Page 37 Student Page 71	Day and Night Sky Teacher Page 41	Arctic Sea Animals Teacher Page 44 Student Page 77	
SOCIAL STUDIES:	Map, Corn Cakes & Maple Syrup Teacher Page 33 Student Page 54	Compare/Contrast First Thanksgiving to Present Day Teacher Page 37 Student Page 72	Map Teacher Page 42 Student Page 54	Map, Eskimo Life Teacher Page 45 Student Page 54	Make Indian Folder, Dress Up and Tell About Different Tribes Teacher Page 50
ART:	Colored Macaroni Necklace Teacher Page 34	Birch Bark Container Teacher Page 38	Thunderbird Mask Teacher Page 42 Student Page 74	Snow Goggles Teacher Page 46	Art Show of Weeks' Projects, Drum/Dance/Chant Performance Teacher Page 50

Turquoise Boy

by Terri Cohlene

READ ALOUD: Whole Group

Before Reading Activity

What kind of gift would you give to people who work hard in the sun? Why? (Discuss.)

This is the story of a gift Turquoise Boy gave to the Navaho Indians who live in the desert. Listen to learn what the gift is and to learn how the Navaho people live.

Teacher Reads Aloud

Turquoise Boy, by Terri Cohlene.

After Reading Activity

What was the gift Turquoise Boy brought? How will horses help the people? What else did you learn about Navaho life? (List responses on board.)

WRITING: Whole Group or Small Groups

Group Activity

Chart Story: "The Navaho Indians." Use ideas listed in the After Reading Activity and have students generate sentences about Navaho life. Arrange the sentences into a chart story.

Pre-Writers: Children copy a sentence from the chart story, then illustrate the sentence.

Beginning Writers: Write a two-sentence story about the Navaho Indians. Draw a picture to go with the story.

Experienced Writers: Write a paragraph about the Navahos. Illustrate it.

READING EXPERIENCE: Whole Group or Small Groups

You Will Need:
- "The Navaho Indians" chart story from Writing Activity
- Student Page 51
- Crayons

Before Reading Activity: What would your day be like if you were a Navaho Indian? Where would you live? What work would you do? What would you eat?

Teacher and Students Read Together: Read together "The Navaho Indians" chart story. Read it through a few times so students can familiarize themselves with it.

After Reading Activity: What might your day be like if you were a Navaho Indian? (Chain student responses on board.)

Example:

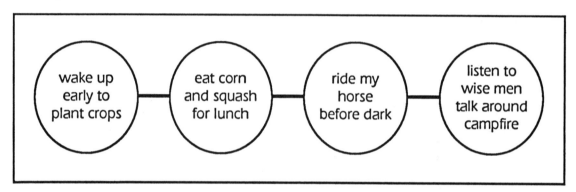

My Day as a Navaho

Student Page 51: Paired Reading—Students write about or draw a picture of what their day would be like as Navaho Indians. Each student then reads his or her story to a partner.

MATH: Whole Group, Small Groups

You Will Need:
- Student Page 52
- Ears of dried Indian corn (one per child or group)

Estimating

Student Page 52: To record work, each child estimates the number of rows of kernels on an ear of corn, then counts the rows. The child continues the activity by following the directions on the worksheet. To extend the activity, have the children add and/or subtract the numbers.

SCIENCE: Whole Group

You Will Need:
- Student Page 53

Corn Cycle

Corn was the main ingredient of the Navaho diet. The Navahos considered corn pollen sacred. Pollen is the dusty substance found on the wavy top of the corn plant. It fertilizes the corn plant so the ears of corn will develop. Without pollen there would be no corn to eat.

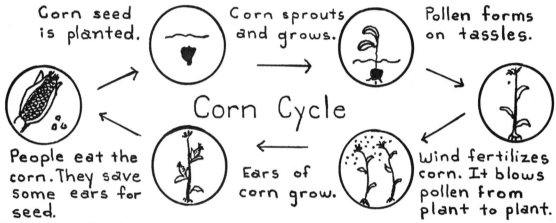

The Corn Cycle

Student Page 53: Children read about and draw pictures of the corn cycle.

SOCIAL STUDIES: Whole Group

You Will Need:
- Student pages 54 and 55

Map

Student Page 54: The Navaho people lived in the desert. They raised crops, had horses, and used what the desert provided for food, clothing, and shelter.

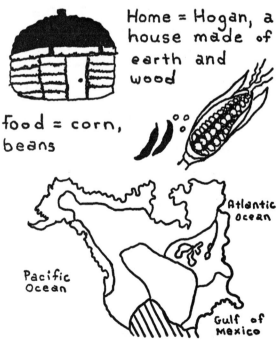

Outline and color the area in which the Navaho and other Southwest Indians lived. Write it in the key and draw the types of homes they lived in and the food they ate.

13

Navaho Life

Student Page 55: Students cut out and paste pictures of items that the Navaho people had around them.

ART: Whole Group

You Will Need:
- 2 sheets construction paper per child
- scissors
- paste

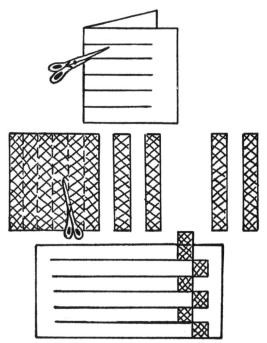

Weaving

1. Students fold one sheet of construction paper in half and cut slots through folded end without cutting through the opposite edge.

2. On the other sheet of paper, cut strips across the width.

3. Weave the strips in and out of the slots. Paste the edges down. The woven paper can be used as a placemat or project folder.

Note: Children can recite a Navaho chant as they work.

"Beauty before me,

Beauty behind me,

Beauty above me and

Beauty beneath me."

When Clay Sings

by Byrd Baylor

READ ALOUD: Whole Group

Before Reading Activity

If you were to make a bowl out of clay, how would you decorate it? Think of things you like very much and how you would draw them on your clay bowl. What would your design say about you? (Discuss.)

This is a story about the clay pottery that Native Americans made a long time ago, and how each piece "sings" with its history.

Teacher Reads Aloud

When Clay Sings, by Byrd Baylor.

After Reading Activity

Think about the design you would give to your piece of pottery. Then listen to what it might say if it could sing. (Discuss.)

WRITING: Whole Group or Small Groups

Group Activity

Draw a clay pot on the board and decorate it with a simple design that the children can describe. As the children describe the pot, write their descriptions on the board. Erase the pot from the board and have the children draw it using only the description. (The teacher may add to the written description if necessary.)

Descriptive Writing

Use Student Page 56.

> **Pre-Writers:** Draw a simple pot and decorate it. Copy and complete the sentences: "My pot is ___(shape)___. It has a ___(decoration)___ on it."

Beginning Writers: Draw the pot and decorate it. On another sheet of paper, write a description of the pot.

Experienced Writers: Draw and decorate a pot. On another sheet of paper, write a complete description of it.

READING EXPERIENCE: Whole Group, Small or Cooperative Groups,

Pairs

You Will Need:
- Student Page 56 from Writing Activity
- crayons
- pencils
- paper

Comprehension

Pre-Writers: Have each child describe his or her pottery drawing without showing it. Instruct the others to draw the pot based on the description.

Beginning Writers: Have each child read his or her written description to the other children, who will then draw the pot described. (The reader may add details to the description if necessary.)

Experienced Writers: Have students fold their Writing papers so that only the description shows. Let each student exchange the description with another student, who will then draw his or her picture from the written description alone.

MATH: Whole Group, Small or Cooperative Groups

You Will Need:
- Student Page 57
- crayons
- scissors
- paste

Symmetry

Student Page 57: When something is symmetric it means that both sides or halves are the same.

To complete the top row of figures on the paper, cut out the pieces on the bottom of the page and paste them in the correct places to make each pot's design symmetric. In the next row, draw in the other half of each pot and its design to make each pot symmetric. Color the pots when you are finished.

SCIENCE: Whole Group

You Will Need:
- Student Page 58
- Book: <u>When Clay Sings</u>
- crayons
- scissors
- paste

Triarama: Animals of the Desert

Student Page 58: Discuss the animals of the desert that are pictured in the book <u>When Clay Sings</u>. Reread the book and have the children look for the many animals mentioned in the story.

1. Have the children color the animal pictures and the background scenery of the triarama on their student pages.
2. Have the children cut out their triaramas.
3. Direct the children step-by-step in how to cut, fold, and paste together the triaramas.
4. Now have the children cut out the animal pictures. Show them how to fold and paste the tabs so the pictures will stand upright on the triaramas.

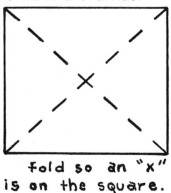

fold so an "x" is on the square.

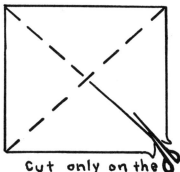

Cut only on the solid line to the middle of the paper.

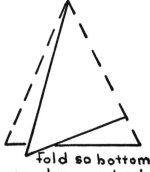

fold so bottom triangles completely overlap. Paste them together. This is the triarama.

SOCIAL STUDIES: Whole Group

You Will Need:
- paper bowls
- plastic spoons
- pencils and crayons
- tortillas
- stirring spoon
- canned chili beans
- large cooking pot
- hot plate

Beans and Tortillas

Beans and corn are the staples of the Southwest Indian diet. The beans are cooked in a large pot. The corn is usually ground into meal and made into a flat round bread called a tortilla.

1. Have the children draw and color symmetric designs to decorate the outsides of their paper bowls.

2. Heat the canned chili beans in the cooking pot. Serve the beans in the children's decorated bowls. Give each child a corn tortilla.

3. Show the children how to tear off a piece of tortilla and use it as a spoon to scoop up the beans.

ART: Whole Group

You Will Need:
- modeling clay for each child
- paper towels
- popsicle sticks (one per child)

Clay Pot

Place the clay on paper towels so desk and table tops won't get dirty. Demonstrate how Indians used the "coil method" to make pottery.

1. Roll the clay into long ropes.

2. Coil one clay rope to form the bottom of the pot.

3. Build up the sides of the pot with additional ropes of clay.

4. Once the pot is formed, use a popsicle stick to smooth the sides and inside.

5. Use the popsicle sticks to make designs on the smoothed sides of the pots.

The Legend of the Bluebonnet

by Tomie dePaola

READ ALOUD: Whole Group

Before Reading Activity

Have you ever given up something special? What was it? Why did you give it up?

This is the story of a Comanche Indian girl who gives up something special to save her people. Listen to learn what she gave up.

Teacher Reads Aloud

The Legend of the Bluebonnet, by Tomie dePaola.

After Reading Activity

What was the special thing that "She-Who-Is-Alone" gave up? What happened at the end of the story?

WRITING: Whole Group or Small Groups

Group Activity

Indian Names: Discuss why the girl was first called "She-Who-Is-Alone," and why her name was changed to "One-Who-Dearly-Loved-Her-People." Discuss what Indian names the children would choose for themselves and why. (Model writing sentences from their ideas.)

Pre-Writers: Use your Indian name to draw a picture of yourself. Copy and complete this sentence:

"My Indian name is_____."

Beginning Writers: Complete the sentence: "My Indian name is

_____. I have this name because

_____."

Use your Indian name to draw a picture of yourself.

Experienced Writers: Write a story that describes your Indian name and how you got it. Draw pictures to illustrate your story.

READING EXPERIENCE: Whole Group or Small Groups

You Will Need:
- 9" x 12" brown construction paper   ■ crayons   ■ scissors

Sign Language Story

Share with the children that the Cheyenne Indians also lived on the plains. They had a written sign language with which to tell stories. Read the different signs listed below.

1. Draw these signs and their meanings on the chalkboard or on a chart.

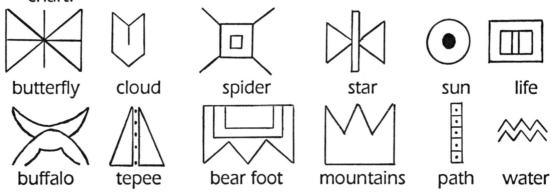

butterfly   cloud   spider   star   sun   life

buffalo   tepee   bear foot   mountains   path   water

Model using these signs to write a story.

2. Have children cut their construction paper as shown below to resemble an animal skin.

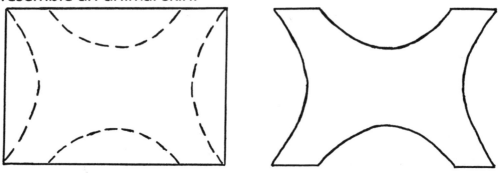

3. Have the children write stories on their "animal skins." Then let them read their stories to someone else or to the class.

MATH: Whole Group or Small Groups

You Will Need:
- Student Page 59
- crayons
- pencils

Fractions ½ and ¼

Student Page 59: The Comanche Indians hung round shields from poles posted around the camp. You may wish to glance again through the story to see the shields.

Draw a circle on the chalkboard to teach the concepts of ½ and ¼.

1. Work through Activity #1 with the class. Draw the design for each section in a square under "Key." In the space next to that design, write the fraction that corresponds to that section. Example:

 = ½

2. Activity #2: Use the Key to design the shield.

3. Activity #3: Design your own shield by dividing the blank circle into ¼ or ½ sections and drawing a design in each section. Fill in the Key to correspond to your design and the corresponding fractions.

SCIENCE: Whole Group

You Will Need:
- Student Page 60
- crayons
- pencils

The Rain Cycle

Student Page 60: Have children draw the rain cycle diagram on their papers.

Discuss as a group the questions at the bottom of the Student Page.

1. A drought occurs when there is not enough rain to sustain plant and animal life.

2. Plants and animals need water in order to survive. If plants die because of drought, animals and people will not only suffer thirst but will also lose their supply of food provided by plants.

3. Discuss other effects of drought.

SOCIAL STUDIES: Whole Group

You Will Need:
- Student page 54
- crayons
- pencils

Map

Student Page 54: Use the map to show where the Plains Indians lived.

Color this region red. Indicate it on the Key and write in "Plains Indians." In the spaces provided, draw pictures of the type of home built by Plains Indians and foods they ate.

Atlantic Ocean

Pacific Ocean

Gulf of Mexico

Food = Buffalo

Homes = tepees made of long poles covered with buffalo hide

ART: Whole Group

You Will Need:
- white paper plates (one for each child)
- scissors
- paste
- feather template (below)

Paper Plate Shields

Plains Indians used shields for protection, identification, and decoration. Each shield had pictures on it that symbolized things that the person liked or did.

Have the children discuss what pictures they would put on their shields and why. Remind them of the Math assignment that used shields to show fractions.

1. Give each child a paper plate, two to four half-circles of differently colored construction paper, scissors, and paste.

2. Instruct the students to cut and paste their shield pieces to the paper plates.

3. Show the children how to cut a strip of paper and paste it on the back of the plate to form a handle.

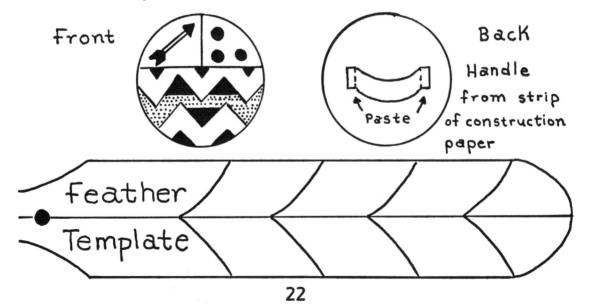

Front

Back

Handle from strip of construction paper

Paste

Feather Template

The Girl Who Loved Wild Horses

by Paul Goble

READ ALOUD: Whole Group

Before Reading Activity

Have you ever loved an animal? What animal was it? (Discuss.)

This story is about a girl who loved horses. Listen to learn what problem she had and what she did to solve it.

Teacher Reads Aloud

The Girl Who Loved Wild Horses, by Paul Goble.

After Reading Activity

What was the problem the girl had? How did she solve it? (Write responses on board.)

Example

Problem: She felt lonely when she was with her family but not when she was with horses.

Solution: She went to live with the horses and returned to visit her family once a year.

WRITING: Whole Group or Small Groups

Group Activity

Character Analysis: Discuss reasons that the girl wanted to stay with the horses. List these on the board. (Model writing full sentences from the list.)

Pre-Writers: Pretend you are the girl. Draw a picture to show why you would want to live with the wild horses. Copy and complete the sentence: "I want to live with the horses because _____."

Beginning Writers: Pretend you are the girl. Write one or two sentences that tell why you want to live with the wild horses. Draw pictures to illustrate your sentences.

Experienced Writers: Pretend you are the girl. Write a one-paragraph story to explain why you want to live with the horses. Illustrate your story.

READING EXPERIENCE: Whole Group, Small or Cooperative Groups

You Will Need:
- Student Page 61   ▪ crayons   ▪ paste
- pencils   ▪ scissors

Summarizing/Finger Puppets

Before Reading Activity: What happened in the story? (Discuss and list events on the board.) Listen to the story again, then write a summary of it.

Teacher Reads Aloud: The Girl Who Loved Wild Horses, by Paul Goble.

After Reading Activity: What happened in the story? (Add events to the list on the board. Make sure to sequence them properly.)

Finger Puppets: Use Student Page 61. Let the children color, cut out, and paste together finger puppets. Have the children act out the story in small groups or in pairs. (This is a creative way to reinforce the skill of summarizing.)

Note: You may wish to display the two songs found at the end of the book on charts for the children to read.

MATH: Whole Group, Small or Cooperative Groups

You Will Need:
- Student Page 62
- crayons
- scissors

Geometric Shapes and Designs

Student Page 62: The Plains Indians made blankets designed with colorful geometric shapes. This activity uses a variety of geometric shapes to replicate some blanket designs.

1. Instruct the children to color the shapes at the bottom of the Student Page:

    ☐ yellow   ☐ red   ◯ blue   △ green

2. Direct the children to cut out the colored shapes.

3. Instruct the children to arrange the shapes on the large blanket in the designs shown at the top. Then have them color the designs at the top appropriately.

Additional Activity: On the backs of their papers, have the children arrange the shapes in their own designs and draw or color them.

SCIENCE: Whole Group

You Will Need:
- Student Page 63   - pencils
- Book: <u>The Girl Who Loved Wild Horses</u>   - crayons

Categorizing Animals of the Plains
Use Student Page 63.

1. Discuss the five main animal groups.

MAMMAL	REPTILE	BIRD	FISH	INSECT
- young born alive - have hair - nurse babies - breathe air	- cold-blooded - most hatch from eggs - scales	- hatch from eggs - have feathers - fly	- live in water - breathe through gills - hatch from eggs	- have six legs - 3 body parts - skeleton on outside

2. Look carefully through the illustrations of the book with the class. Write the names of the different animals seen on each page under the correct heading on the board. Discuss why each animal belongs under that heading. Example:

MAMMAL				REPTILE	BIRD	FISH	INSECT
rabbits	moose	bear	horses	lizards	quail	fish	butterflies
badgers	elk	antelope		turtles	owl		
prairie dogs	deer	mice			hawk		

Students draw and write the names of animals they recognized in the book under each category listed. Example:

Mammal

horse

SOCIAL STUDIES: Whole Group or Small Groups

You Will Need:
- 12" x 18" white construction paper (one piece per child)
- crayons and markers

Indian Poster

Have the children make posters that show what they have learned about the Plains Indians (and/or the Southwest Indians).

ART: Whole Group

You Will Need:
- plastic drinking straws (three per child)
- straight pins (one per child)
- paper towels
- 9" x 12" white or tan construction paper (one piece per child)
- modeling clay
- paste, scissors, crayons

Tepee Model

Have children cover their desks with paper towels so desks won't get messy with clay.

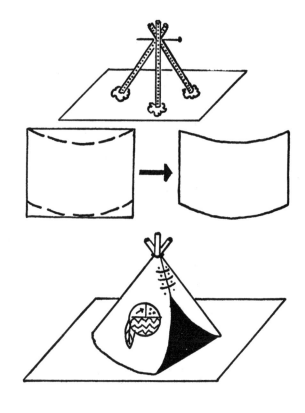

1. Secure three plastic straws in three small balls of clay. Connect the straws at the top with a straight pin.

2. Instruct each child to cut the piece of construction paper as shown at right. This shape should fit around the tepee frame. The child can further tailor it to fit if necessary.

3. Let the children decorate their papers. They may use some of the signs they have already learned, or look through the book The Girl Who Loved Wild Horses for ideas.

4. Show the children how to fit the tepee cover over the frame and paste it in place.

Note: While the children work, they can sing or chant this Cheyenne song: " Nothing lives long;
Only the earth
And the mountains."

Dancing Drum

by Terri Cohlene

READ ALOUD: Whole Group

Before Reading Activity

Have you ever wondered what makes the sun shine or the weather change? What do you think causes these things? (Discuss.)

This is a Cherokee legend about the sun and the weather. Listen to the Cherokee explanation.

Teacher Reads Aloud

Dancing Drum, by Terri Cohlene.

After Reading Activity

How did the Cherokee people explain the sun and weather? (Discuss.)

WRITING: Whole Group or Small Groups

Group Activity

Predicting Outcomes: Talk about what would happen if the sun didn't shine. (Chain responses on board.)

Example:

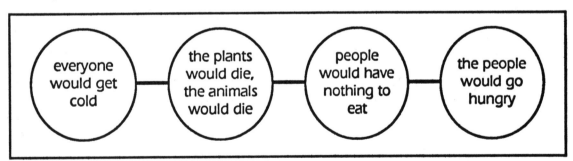

Pre-Writers: Copy one sentence from the chain on the board. Draw a picture of it.

Beginning Writers: Draw pictures to illustrate three things that would happen if the sun didn't shine. Write a sentence to describe each picture.

Experienced Writers: Write a chain of events that would happen if the sun didn't shine. Illustrate each event.

READING EXPERIENCE: Whole Group, Small or Cooperative Groups

You Will Need:
- Student Page 64
- crayons
- Book: Dancing Drum
- pencils
- scissors

Summarizing

Before Reading Activity: What events took place in the story Dancing Drum? (List on board in proper sequence, making sure children direct the order.)

Teacher Reads Aloud: Dancing Drum, by Terri Cohlene.

After Reading Activity: What happened in the story? Read through the list already on the board, then have children add other events. Model writing sentences from the list, keeping them short enough to fit along the snake on the Student Page.

Student Page 64: Have each child write a summary of the story along the body of the snake. Each child may then color it, cut it out, and read it to a partner.

ACTIVITY CHOICES: Small or Cooperative Groups

Children choose one or two of these activities to do in a 1 to 1½ hour block of time.

Paper Plate Masks

Most Indian tribes made masks for ceremonial dances and other rituals. These were usually made of wood, leather, beads, and feathers. They often represented either an animal spirit or a god.

You Will Need:
- paper plates (one per child)
- paper hole punch
- strong string or yarn
- scissors
- construction paper (many colors)
- paste
- crayons

Note: Beads, feathers, or ribbons can add delightful touches to this project.

1. Children draw eyes and mouth on paper plates and cut these out.

2. They then decorate the plates with bits of colored paper, crayons, and any other material available.

3. Punch holes in the sides of each mask and tie a length of yarn to each side to fasten mask to the child's head. Let the children practice a chant/dance together with their masks on.

Act Out Indian Stories

You will need all of the books read this week: <u>Turquoise</u>, by Cohlene; <u>When Clay Sings</u>, by Baylor; <u>The Legend of the Bluebonnet</u>, by dePaola; <u>The Girl Who Loved Wild Horses</u>, by Goble; and <u>Dancing Drum</u>, by Cohlene.

Let the children reread the stories and make up skits to act them out. Or, encourage them to make up their own Indian stories to act out. Arrange a time for the children to present their plays.

Travois Model

Travois were used by the Plains Indians as a means of transporting their belongings. These were used on both horses and dogs.

You Will Need:
- modeling clay • straight pins
- plastic drinking straws • string

1. Make a clay model of a horse or dog.

2. Fashion a travois made of drinking straws over the animal's shoulders and neck. Tie these together with string.

3. Use short lengths of straw fixed with pins to make a small platform on the back of the travois.

SOCIAL STUDIES: Whole or Small Group

You Will Need:
- Student Pages 54 and 65

Map

Use the map (Student Page 54) to show where the Southeast Indians lived. Color this region green and mark it on the key.

Homes = Palisade huts of grass and mud with domed roofs. Grouped into villages.

Cherokee History

Student Page 65: Read to the children or help them to read the information about the Cherokee Indians.

Food = Variety of foods from farming and hunting.

ART: Whole Group

You Will Need:
- 1 large paper bag per child
- scissors
- crayons

Buckskin Vest

The Cherokee people wore clothes made out of the skins of deer they hunted. Let the children make their own "buckskin" vests.

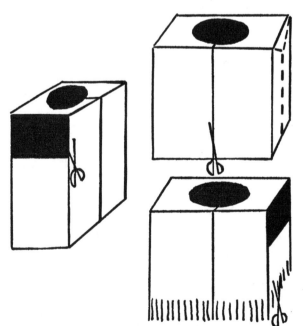

1. Cut a line down the middle of one side of the bag and on to the bottom. Cut a circle out of the bottom of the bag to form a hole for the neck.

2. Cut square holes in each side next to the bottom to serve as arm holes.

3. Turn the bag inside-out to eliminate any writing showing on the outside.

4. Have children make fringe along the bottom with their scissors. Then let them decorate their vests with crayons.

The Rough-Face Girl

by Rafe Martin

READ ALOUD: Whole Group

Before Reading Activity

Do you know the story of Cinderella? (Recount it if some children aren't familiar with it.)

This is an Algonquin Indian tale that resembles the story of Cinderella. Listen to all the ways it is like Cinderella.

Teacher Reads Aloud

The Rough-Face Girl, by Rafe Martin.

After Reading Activity

How is this story like Cinderella? (Discuss.)

WRITING: Whole Group, Small or Cooperative Groups

Group Activity

Similarities and Differences: In what ways is the story The Rough-Face Girl the same as the story of Cinderella? How is it different? (List on board.)

Example: Same: bad sisters; happy ending
             Different: man not a prince; no glass slipper, etc.

Pre-Writers: Draw two pictures, one to show how this story is the same as the story of Cinderella, and one to show how this story is different from the story of Cinderella.

Beginning Writers: Write a sentence that tells one way this story is the same as the story of Cinderella and a sentence that tells one way the two stories are different. Draw a picture to go with each sentence.

Experienced Writers: Write a paragraph to describe two or three ways the stories are similar and different. Draw pictures to illustrate your paragraph.

READING EXPERIENCE: Whole Group, Small or Cooperative Groups

You Will Need:
- Student Page 66   ▪ Book: The Rough-Face Girl

Story Frame

This activity studies the character, problem, and solution presented in the story.

Before Reading Activity: I'm going to read The Rough-Face Girl again. Listen to identify all the characters in the story. Listen especially for the problem one character has and how that problem is solved.

Teacher Reads Aloud: The Rough-Face Girl, by Rafe Martin.

After Reading Activity: Who were the characters in the story? What was the problem the main character had? How was that problem solved? (List responses on board. Then work with the children to condense both the problem and the solution into one or two sentences.)

Student Page 66: Children illustrate and write about the main character, the problem, and the solution.

MATH: Whole Group, Small or Cooperative Groups

You Will Need:
- Student Page 67   • crayons

Patterning

Student Page 67: This higher-thinking activity will help children to discern patterns.

Discuss patterning and how it works. Have the children complete the patterns on the Student Page. Then let the children use the shapes to design necklaces in the space provided.

Another Challenge

Once they've completed the patterns, have the children color in the shapes as follows:

$\triangle$ = red $\square$ = blue $\bigcirc$ = yellow

$\varobslash$ = orange $\bigtriangledown$ = purple $\bigcap$ = green

SCIENCE: Whole Group

You Will Need:
- Student Page 68   • crayons

Uses For Birch Bark

Student Page 68: Birch bark was used by the Algonquin Indians for many things. Read to the children, or allow them to read, about the many uses Algonquins had for birch bark. Let them follow the directions to color or add additional items to the pictures.

SOCIAL STUDIES: Whole Group, Small or Cooperative Groups

Map

Student Page 54: Use the map to locate where the Algonquin Indians lived. Color the region blue and mark it on the key.

Discuss how Algonquin homes and foods were similar to and different from those of the other Indians studied (especially the Cherokee). In the spaces provided, draw pictures of and describe Algonquin homes and foods.

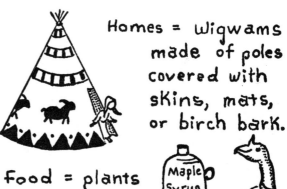

Homes = Wigwams made of poles covered with skins, mats, or birch bark.

Food = plants gathered and animals hunted in woods.

Corn Cakes and Maple Syrup

You Will Need:

- Student Page 54
- corn meal
- maple syrup
- paper plates
- pancake turner
- water
- plastic forks
- all-purpose flour
- baking powder
- electric skillet
- bowl
- spoon
- eggs
- sugar
- butter
- salt
- milk

1. In a bowl, mix: 1 cup yellow corn meal, 1 tsp. salt, 2 Tblsp. sugar.

2. Stir in: 1 cup boiling water. Cover and let stand 10 minutes.

3. In a separate bowl, beat: 1 egg, ½ cup milk, 2 Tblsp. melted butter. Add to the corn meal.

4. Stir into batter: ½ cup all-purpose flour, 2 tsp. baking powder.

5. Drop by large spoonfuls onto hot, lightly-greased skillet. When bubbles begin to appear, use pancake turner to flip over. Cook other side till golden and easy to lift with turner. Remove from skillet.

Makes about 12 four-inch corn cakes. Serve with maple-flavored syrup.

Note: Prepare one batch each for three or four groups, so every child will be able to participate in the preparation.

ART: Whole Group

You Will Need:
- macaroni
- four bowls or jars
- strainer
- food coloring: blue, red, green, yellow
- string
- cookie sheets
- paper cups
- paper towels

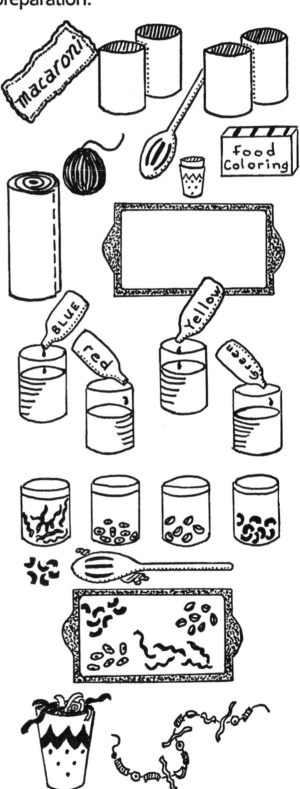

Colored Macaroni Necklace

To color macaroni:

1. Mix different colors of food coloring with small amounts of water in separate containers to make a strong solution of each color.

2. Soak batches of macaroni in each color solution till color is absorbed (a few minutes).

3. Remove macaroni with slotted spoon to drain.

4. Spread macaroni on cookie sheets. Allow to dry overnight. (Leave some macaroni its natural color.)

Give each child a string about 30 inches long and a cup of the multi-colored macaroni.

Let each child make a necklace.

The Star Maiden

by Barbara Juster Esbensen

READ ALOUD: Whole Group

Before Reading Activity

Think of some of the pretty things in nature that you enjoy. What are they? (Discuss.)

This story is about a Star Maiden who wanted to become something beautiful on earth. Listen to learn what she becomes and the problems she encounters.

Teacher Reads Aloud

The Star Maiden, by Barbara Juster Esbensen.

Note: You may wish to point out the dome-shaped wigwams pictured in this story.

After Reading Activity

What beautiful thing did the Star Maiden become? What problems did she have? (Discuss.)

WRITING: Whole Group, Small or Cooperative Groups

Group Activity

If you were a Star Maiden, what beautiful thing would you want to become? Why? (List ideas on board.)

Pre-Writers: Draw a picture of what you would become if you were a Star Maiden. Copy and complete the sentence: "I would become a _____ because _____."

Beginning Writers: Write a story to describe what you would become and why. Draw a picture to go with your story.

Experienced Writers: Write a story in which you are a Star Maiden. Describe what you chose to become and explain why. Illustrate your story.

READING EXPERIENCE: Whole Group, Small or Cooperative Groups

You Will Need:
- Student Page 69   ■ scissors ■ crayons ■ pencils
- Book: The Star Maiden

Foldbook

Before Reading Activity: What happened in the beginning, middle, and end of the story? (List on board.) Listen to the beginning, middle, and end as I read the story again.

Teacher Reads Aloud: <u>The Star Maiden</u>, by Barbara Juster Esbensen.

After Reading Activity: What happened at the beginning, middle, and end of the story? (Add to the list on board.) Encourage children to condense the information into a single phrase. (Model using those phrases to write a sentence or two.)

Student Page 69: Children cut and fold the foldbook. They then draw pictures and write descriptions of the beginning, middle, and end of the story.

MATH: Whole Group, Small or Cooperative Groups

You Will Need:
- Student Page 70 - crayons - pencils - scissors

Moccasin Measuring

The Algonquin Indians made moccasins out of deer skins. They decorated them with beads and colorful designs. The Indians learned to move very quietly in their moccasins by walking on the outside edges of their feet. (Children may wish to practice walking like this.)

Student Page 70:

1. Direct the children to trace around one of their feet in the box provided at the bottom of the page. Have them cut out the foot shape and put their names on the back. Let the children decorate the "feet" to look like moccasins.

2. Teach the children how to use their moccasins to measure the lengths and widths of the things specified on the page. Encourage them to use fractions. (Example: desk = 5½ moccasins)

SCIENCE: Whole Group

You Will Need:
- Student Page 71   - crayons

Parts of a Flower

Flowers have six parts.

1. The **roots** anchor the plant and absorb nutrients and water from the soil. (Note: Though a water lily floats on top of the water, its roots are anchored into the soil at the bottom of the lake, and its stem leads to the floating leaves and flower.)

2. The **stem** brings nutrients from the roots to the leaves and flowers.

3. The **leaves** collect sunlight. Photosynthesis takes place in the leaves, turning light energy from the sun into nutrients that feed the plant and make it grow.

4. When the plant is ready to make a flower, a bud forms.

5. Most flowers have many brightly colored petals that surround the stamen and pistil. The colored petals attract bees and other insects to pollinate the flower.

6. The **stamens** produce the pollen in the flower. Stamens come in many different shapes.

7. **Pistils** are the seed-producing parts of the flower. When the pistil is pollinated, the plant is ready to make seeds so another plant can grow.

Student Page 71: Have the children follow these instructions:
- Color the roots brown.
- Color the leaves green.
- Color the stem light-green.
- Color the petals yellow.
- Color the stamen orange.
- Color the pistil red.

Next instruct children to draw their own flowers, label the parts, and write descriptions below their drawings.

SOCIAL STUDIES: Whole Group

You Will Need:
- Student Page 72

Compare/Contrast the First Thanksgiving

It was the Algonquin Indians who helped the Pilgrims at Plymouth Colony in 1620. They helped the colonists plant crops, gather food, and hunt in the woods. The first winter was very difficult for the

Pilgrims. Many people got sick and died. Without the help of the Indians, many more would have suffered. After the first harvest, the Pilgrims and Indians shared a feast of thanksgiving to celebrate their survival through the hardship.

1. Discuss the kinds of food that the Pilgrims and Indians had available to them (corn, beans, pumpkin, wild turkey, deer, rabbit, squirrel, cranberries, clams, fish). These are some of the foods the Pilgrims and Indians shared at the first Thanksgiving.

2. Discuss the types of utensils they might have used.
   (Indians: wooden plates, shell bowls and scoops, bowls, cups and ladles formed from gourds, and stone knives.
   Pilgrims: iron pots, wooden spoons, metal knives, forks, and spoons.)

3. Discuss the similarities and differences of the first Thanksgiving and present-day Thanksgiving celebrations.

Student Page 72: The children draw a picture of the first Thanksgiving and their own Thanksgiving celebrations. They then draw and write about things that are the same and different between the two.

ART: Whole Group

You Will Need:
- medium-sized brown paper bags (one per child)
- paper hole punch
- strong brown string or yarn
- crayons and scissors

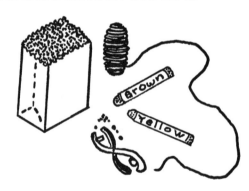

Birch Bark Container

Algonquin Indians used decorated containers made of sewn birch bark to hold many things. To make a paper bag replica, follow these instructions.

1. Texture paper bags to resemble birch bark: Draw dark lines with brown and yellow crayons.

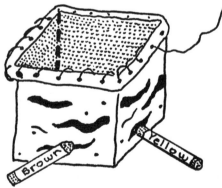

2. Carefully roll down the top edges two or three times. Punch holes evenly along the rolled edge.

3. Thread string or yarn through holes around the top.

Note: If bags have writing on them, turn them inside out.

How Raven Brought Light To People

by Ann Dixon

READ ALOUD: Whole Group

Before Reading Activity

This is a Northwest Indian legend that tells how the sun, moon, and stars came to be.

Listen carefully for clues about where the Northwest Indians lived, what their houses looked like, and other facts about their way of life.

Teacher Reads Aloud

How Raven Brought Light to People, by Ann Dixon.

After Reading Activity

What can you tell about the Northwest Indians? (List responses on board.)

WRITING: Whole Group or Small Groups

Group Activity

Writing From Fact: Use information generated during the After Reading Activity to write a chart story about the Northwest Indians.

Pre-Writers: Copy a sentence from the chart story. Draw a picture to go with it.

Beginning Writers: Write two sentences about the Northwest Indians. Draw a picture to go with each sentence.

Experienced Writers: Write a short report about the Northwest Indians. Draw pictures to illustrate your story.

READING EXPERIENCE: Whole Group, Small or Cooperative Groups

You Will Need:
- paper   - pencils   - crayons

Predicting Outcomes

Discuss how life would be different if there were no sun. List the student ideas on the board. Number each idea by order of cause and effect sequence. Then use a chain diagram to illustrate what would happen.

Example:

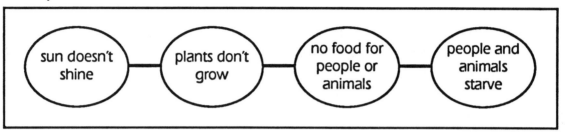

Instruct the children to draw and write their own chain of ideas about what life would be like without the sun. They may then read their chain to a partner.

MATH: Whole Group, Small or Cooperative Groups

You Will Need:
- Student Page 73
- pencils
- rulers or straight edges (one per child)
- scissors
- transparent tape
- crayons

Following Directions

The following exercise introduces children to using graph paper, using a straight edge to draw lines of specified length, and following oral directions.

Student Page 73: Read aloud to the class the following directions.

1. Put your pencil on the dot that says "Start." Place your ruler along that horizontal line on your graph paper. Count 5 spaces to the right. Put a dot there. Draw a line between the two dots.

2. Move your pencil down to dot #2. Place your ruler along that horizontal line. Count over 5 spaces to the right. Put a dot there. Draw a line between the dots.

3. Put your pencil on dot #3. Place your ruler along that horizontal line. Count over 11 spaces to the right. Draw a line between dots #3 and #6.

4. Move down to dot #4. Put your pencil on it. Place your ruler along that horizontal line. Count over 11 spaces to the right. Put a dot there. Draw a line between the dots.

5. Put your pencil on dot #5. Place your ruler along that line. Find dot #8. Draw a line between dots #5 and #8.

How Raven Brought Light To People

6. Turn your paper sideways and find dot #6. Put your pencil on it. Place your ruler along that line. Count over 3 spaces to the right. There should already be a dot there. Draw a line between dot #6 and that dot.

7. Find dot #7. Put your pencil on it and place your ruler along that line. Find dot #8. Draw a line between dots #7 and #8.

8. Move your pencil to dot #9. It is the same place we started. This is the last line you will draw. Place your ruler along that line and find dot #5. Draw a line between dots #9 and #5.

Make One of Raven's Boxes

Remind children that the Northwest Indians made their boxes out of wood and decorated them with bright colors.

1. Have children color all the pictures. They then may cut out the sun, moon, and stars to put in their boxes when finished.

2. Have the children follow the lines they drew in the Following Directions activity to cut out the perimeters of their boxes.

3. Fold along the dotted lines.

4. Form into a box shape and tape the edges together with transparent tape. Children can put the sun, moon, and stars in their Northwest Indians boxes.

SCIENCE: Whole Group

You Will Need:
- 12" x 9" white construction paper (one piece per child)
- 9" x 6" dark blue construction paper (one piece per child)
- paste
- crayons   ▪ straight pins (one per child)

Day and Night Sky

Discuss what the children see in the sky during the day and during the night. Why is it important to have both day and night?

1. Have the children paste the dark blue paper over one half of the white paper.

2. Instruct them to draw what the sky looks like during the day and to write something they do during the day that can't be done at night.

3. Direct the children to draw the moon in the night sky on the dark blue sides of their papers. Instead of drawing stars, have the children poke through the paper with the straight pins so they can see through it when it's held up to light. You may wish to teach a few basic constellations that the children can design in their skies.

SOCIAL STUDIES: Whole Group, Small or Cooperative Groups

Map

Use the map on Student Page 54 to indicate where the Northwest Indians live. Color this region purple and mark it on the key. Draw pictures and write descriptions of the homes and foods of Northwest Indians.

Homes = long houses made of wooden planks

Foods = seafood, salmon, food hunted and gathered in the forest

ART: Whole Group

You Will Need:
- Student Page 74
- scissors
- paste
- crayons

Thunderbird Mask

The Northwest Indians used many types of masks in their religious ceremonies. One of the most impressive masks was that of the Thunderbird who lived high in the mountains and brought thunder, lightning, and rain clouds to the people.

1. Have the children color and cut out the mask on Student Page 74. They also cut out two strips to form the headband.

2. Show the children how to fold the masks and paste the tips of the beak together. (Stapling or taping the tips may work best.)

3. Paste or staple one headband strip to each side of the mask. Have children try on masks. Overlap the strips in back to fit the head. Paste or staple together.

42

Song of Sedna

by Robert San Souci

READ ALOUD: Whole Group

Before Reading Activity

Eskimos depended on the sea for their food and clothing. They believed in a goddess of the sea named Sedna who could protect the fishermen and hunters from harm.

This is the story about how Sedna became the sea goddess. Listen to learn how she came to live under the sea.

Teacher Reads Aloud

Song of Sedna, by Robert San Souci.

After Reading Activity

How did Sedna come to live in the sea? Is this a real or make-believe story? How can you tell? (Discuss.)

WRITING: Whole Group or Small Groups

Group Activity

Discuss what kinds of things may have happened after the end of the story. (Model using student responses to write sentences.)

Pre-Writers: Draw a picture of what you think happened after the end of the story. Copy the appropriate sentence from the board.

Beginning Writers: Write a sentence to describe what you think happened after the end of the story. Draw a picture to go with it.

Experienced Writers: List some ideas about what happened after the end of the story. Use your list to write a story. Illustrate your story.

READING EXPERIENCE: Whole Group, Small or Cooperative Groups

You Will Need:
- Student page 75
- crayons
- scissors
- paste

Sequencing

1. With the students' help, list all the events of the story on the board.

2. Arrange the events in the proper sequence.

3. Condense all the happenings into three major events. Read these aloud so students understand the sequence as well as the words.

Student Page 75: Children cut out the three events written on the bottom of the page and paste them to the spaces numbered 1, 2, and 3 in their proper sequence. They then draw a picture to illustrate each event.

MATH: Whole Group, Small or Cooperative Groups

You Will Need:
- Student Page 76 ▪ pencils ▪ crayons

Understanding Temperature

This exercise will help children learn to read a Fahrenheit thermometer and to understand what temperature means.

Teach the children how to read a thermometer in 5-degree intervals. Discuss the kinds of clothes the children would wear for different temperatures.

Water freezes at 32°F. The Eskimos live where it is very cold. Often the temperature is below zero. They wear clothing made of animal fur.

Student Page 76: In Activity #1, children read the temperatures and write them down. They then circle the words that describe temperatures. For Activity #2 the children should mark the thermometers to indicate the correct temperatures, then draw and list appropriate clothing.

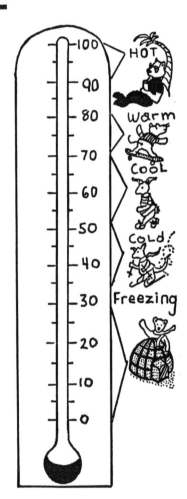

SCIENCE: Whole Group

You Will Need:
- Student Page 77 ▪ watercolor paint (blue) and brushes ▪ crayons

Arctic Sea Animals

Eskimos depended on Arctic sea animals for food and clothing. Discuss specific characteristics of each Arctic sea animal. Have the children locate them on their papers.

<u>Walrus</u>
- Has two long ivory tusks, two flippers, and thick, wiry whiskers on face.
- Eskimos used the ivory to make fish hooks, harpoons, needles, utensils, and decorations.
- They used the skin to cover their boats (called umiaks), to make shoes (called mukluks), and to make snow shoes.

<u>Killer Whales, Humpback Whales, Narwhal</u>
- Whale meat and blubber was a favorite Eskimo food.
- Bones were used to make tools and utensils.
- Blubber was rendered into oil for use in lamps.

<u>Seals</u>
- Eskimos ate the meat and used the soft fur for clothing.
- Fat was used to make oil for lamps.

Student Page 77: Each child colors the Arctic sea animals with heavy crayon. They may wish to add additional fish to the picture. Once the coloring is complete, the child paints a watercolor wash over the picture to give it an ocean effect.

Homes = igloos during winter, sod houses during summer

SOCIAL STUDIES: Whole Group

You Will Need:
- Student Page 54   ■ pencils and paper

Food = Arctic sea life

Map

Use the map on Student Page 54 to indicate where the Eskimos live. Color the region brown and mark it on the key. Draw pictures of the homes they built and foods they ate and describe these things in the spaces provided.

Eskimo Life

Children will learn about Eskimo life. Then in small groups they will work out pantomimes about life as an Eskimo.

- Eskimos lived in dome-shaped igloos made of blocks of ice. The doorway was small and they had to crawl in and out so cold air wouldn't get inside.
- They traveled over the ice and snow on sleds pulled by dog teams.
- In their boats, called "umiaks," they paddled into the ocean to hunt walruses, seals, and whales, which they killed with harpoons.
- The women skinned the animals. They scraped the furs to make them

soft. They then used ivory or bone needles to sew the furs together.

- Ice Fishing: Eskimos cut holes in the ice and dropped lines into the water to catch fish.
- Eskimos didn't use plates and forks to eat; they used only knives. Meat would be cut into strips, which a person would bite into, then cut off with a knife.
- Eskimos wore heavy pants and parkas made of animal skins, thick boots called "mukluks," and warm, fur-lined mittens.
- They cooked over small fires which they built in the center of the igloo, used small oil lamps for light, and slept on beds made of animal fur.

ART: Whole Group

You Will Need:
- tagboard templates for snow goggles (below)
- tan construction paper
- string and scissors
- paste

Snow Goggles

To prevent snow blindness, Eskimos carved snow goggles that had narrow slits for the eyes. The goggles protected their eyes from bright light reflected by the snow.

<u>Snow Goggles</u>: Trace around the snow goggle template on the tan construction paper. Cut it out. Punch holes in the ends and tie string through each hole. Fasten it around the head.

While working, children may wish to chant Sedna's song.

Brother Eagle, Sister Sky

by Susan Jeffers

READ ALOUD: Whole Group

Before Reading Activity

Native Americans believed that people belonged to the land. It was hard for them to understand how land could be sold or owned by someone.

This story is based on the words of a great Northwest Indian Chief named Seattle. Listen to how he speaks about the environment. Look at the pictures to see Native Americans from the many regions we have studied.

Teacher Reads Aloud

Brother Eagle, Sister Sky, by Susan Jeffers.

After Reading Activity

How did Chief Seattle speak of the environment? How are his ideas the same as those who talk about the environment today? (Discuss.) Look through the pictures of the book and discuss how many different Native American regions are pictured.

WRITING: Whole Group or Small Groups

Group Activity

Letter Writing: If Chief Seattle were here today, what would you tell him about the environment? (List ideas on board.)

Introduce letter format and use sentences dictated by students to write a letter to Chief Seattle.

Pre-Writers: Draw a picture for Chief Seattle that tells something about the environment. Copy and complete this letter:

"Dear Chief Seattle,

The environment is _____ because_____ .

Your friend, _____"

Beginning Writers: Write a letter to Chief Seattle telling him about our environment. Draw a picture to go with your letter.

Experienced Writers: Write a letter to Chief Seattle about the state of our environment and what is being done to help it. Illustrate your letter.

ACTIVITY CHOICES: Small or Cooperative Groups

Children choose one or two of these activities to do in a 1 to 1½ hour block of time.

Sugar Cube Igloo

Eskimos built igloos out of blocks of ice to live in during the harsh winter months.

You Will Need:
- 2–5 boxes of sugar cubes
- 1-cup plastic margarine tubs (one per child/igloo)
- 9" x 12" piece of cardboard
- glue or tape
- white construction paper

1. Cover cardboard with white construction paper and tape it down.

2. Tape inverted margarine tub to covered cardboard to prevent it from moving while constructing the igloo.

3. To make the doorway, cut out a 2" x 2" square piece of white construction paper. Fold the paper so it forms an arch and attach it to the margarine tub.

4. Place sugar cubes around the base of the margarine tub. Build them up layer by layer, using glue or tape to hold together, until the tub and doorway arch are covered.

Indian Pudding

Algonquin Indians originally made this dish. The Pilgrims tried it, liked it, and made it themselves. People still call it Indian Pudding.

You will need:

½ gallon milk
1⅓ cup corn meal
3 cups dark molasses
1 cup butter
2 Tbsp. salt
2 Tbsp. ginger
4 well-beaten eggs

2 cups raisins
1 Tbsp. cinnamon
1 cup sugar
8 cups thinly sliced apples
large cooking pot
hot plate
cutting board

4 well-greased baking dishes
stirring and serving spoons
measuring cups and spoons
small mixing bowl (for eggs)
sharp knife (to slice apples)
paper bowls
plastic spoons

1. Boil the milk in the large cooking pot over medium heat, stirring frequently. Be careful not to scorch.

2. Stir in corn meal. Cook over medium heat 10-15 minutes, stirring occasionally.

3. Stir in molasses. Cook for about 5 minutes more, stirring occasionally.

4. Remove from heat and stir in butter, salt, ginger, eggs, raisins, cinnamon, sugar, and apples.

5. Pour the batter into four well-greased baking pans. Bake at 325° for 1½ to 2 hours.

6. Serve warm in paper bowls. Eat with plastic spoons.

Drums, Rattles, Dances, and Chants

You Will Need:

- assorted coffee cans, pill bottles, film canisters, etc., with plastic lids
- assorted beans, seeds, pebbles (for rattles)
- construction paper
- paste
- scissors
- crayons
- felt pens

1. Coffee cans with lids become drums and can be decorated by covering with construction paper and coloring with felt pens.

2. Rattles are made by putting beans/seeds/corn into smaller cans or canisters and shaking them.

3. The children can practice chants.

Algonquin
"A ring of silver foxes,
 A mist of silver foxes,
 Come and sit around
 the hunting moon."

Navaho
"Beauty before me,
 Beauty behind me,
 Beauty above me, and
 Beauty beneath me."

Cheyenne
"Nothing lives long,
 Only the earth
 And the mountains."

4. A Cherokee dance is done by moving heel-toe, heel-toe around in a circle. A Northwest Indian chieftain once said, "I dance because I am rich."

SOCIAL STUDIES: Whole Group

You Will Need:
- 12" x 18" construction paper
- crayons
- stapler

Folder

Construct a Native American folder to hold all the work done during the two weeks. Staple the work inside the folder to make a book.

Dress-Up

Children dress up as their favorite Native Americans and tell about their tribes. They can use some of the art projects done during this unit and supplement these with other items or pieces of clothing brought from home.

ART: Whole Group

You Will Need:
- art projects done during the two weeks
- drums and rattles from morning activity

Art Show

Have an art show to display the projects made during the two weeks.

These projects can be displayed on partitions (made from painted refrigerator boxes), bulletin boards, doors, and windows. Some items can be worn by the students (necklaces, masks, etc.).

Invite parents, school officials, and other classes to the exhibit. Let the children explain their projects and what they've learned.

Drum, Dance, and Chant Performance

Using the morning activity, let the children prepare a performance to demonstrate Native American music, chants, and dances. Choose some children to explain the performances to their audience.

My Day As A Navaho

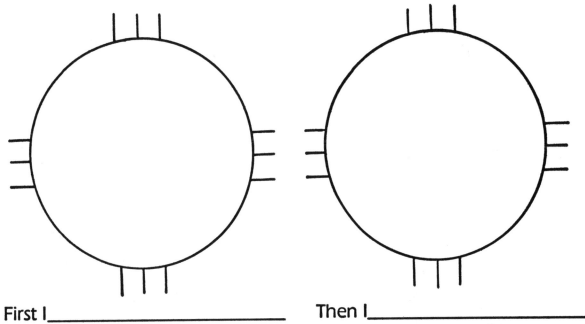

First I_____

_____

_____

Then I_____

_____

_____

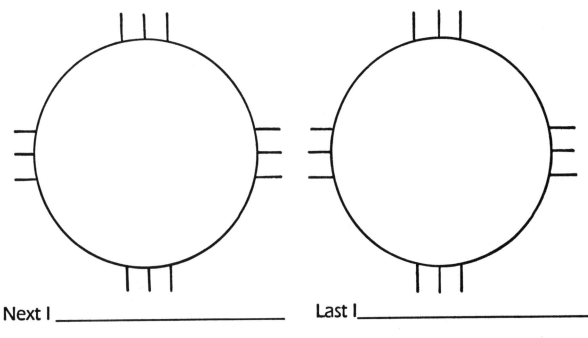

Next I _____

_____

_____

Last I_____

_____

_____

Name _____

Estimation

1. Estimate the number of rows of kernels on the ear of corn. _____

   Count the number of rows of kernels. _____

2. Estimate the number of kernels of corn in one row. _____

   Count the number of kernels of corn in one row. _____

3. What colors are on your ear of corn? _____

   _____

4. ☐ Color the box one of these colors.

   ☐ Color this box another of these colors.

5. Estimate the number of colors in one row. _____

   Count the number of colors in one row. _____

6. Draw your ear of corn below.

The Corn Cycle

Draw a picture of each step of the corn cycle.

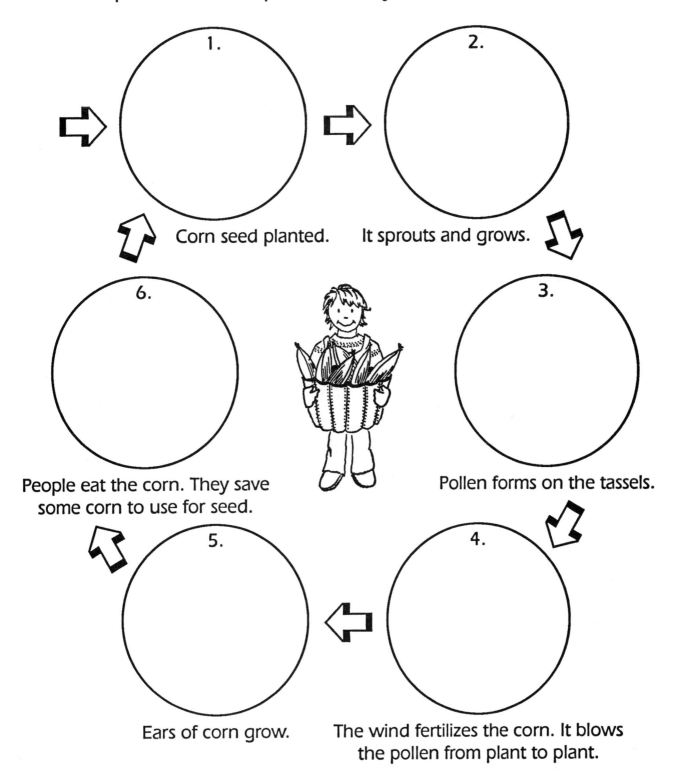

1.

2.

Corn seed planted.   It sprouts and grows.

6.

3.

People eat the corn. They save some corn to use for seed.   Pollen forms on the tassels.

5.

4.

Ears of corn grow.   The wind fertilizes the corn. It blows the pollen from plant to plant.

Name _____

Map

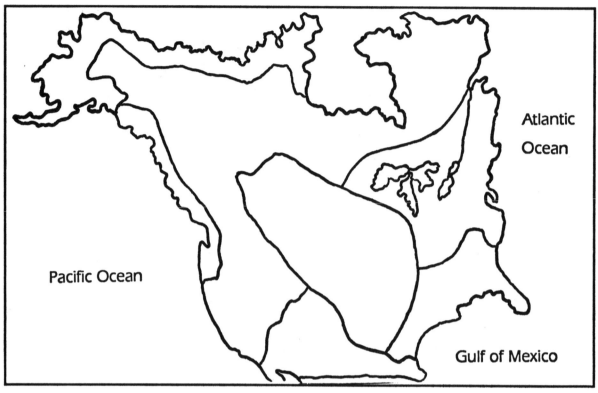

Atlantic Ocean

Pacific Ocean

Gulf of Mexico

KEY	REGION	HOME Picture	Description	FOOD Picture	Description

Name _____

Navaho Life

Cut and paste the things the Navaho people had around them.

Name _____

Descriptive Writing

Draw and describe a clay pot.

Symmetry

1. Cut out the pieces below the dotted line and paste them in the right places.

2. Draw in the other side of each pot and color the completed pots.

Name _____

Triarama: Animals of the Desert

1. Color the animals and the scenery.
2. Cut out and paste the triarama together.
3. Cut out and paste the animals to the triarama.

Paste   Paste   paste   Paste   ←fold

Name _____

Fractions

Activity #1

KEY

▢ = _____

▢ = _____

▢ = _____

▢ = _____

▢ = _____

▢ = _____

▢ = _____

Activity #2
Follow the directions
to make a shield.

Activity #3
Design your own shield.
Make a KEY to go with it.

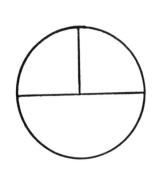

KEY

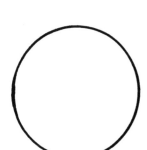

▦ = ¼

⊡ = ½

▣ = ¼

KEY

▢ = ____

▢ = ____

▢ = ____

The Rain Cycle

Draw the rain cycle.

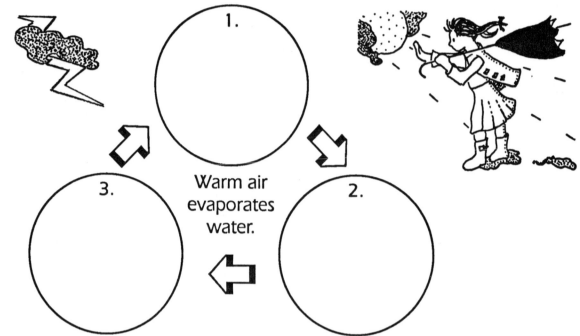

1.

3.

Warm air
evaporates
water.

2.

Evaporated water condenses
and falls as rain.

Warm air rises and
meets cold air.

1. What is a drought? _____

_____

_____

2. Why is a drought bad?_____

_____

_____

3. What else happens when it doesn't rain? Why? _____

_____

_____

_____

Summarizing/Finger Puppets

Color, cut out, and paste together the finger puppets. Act out the story.

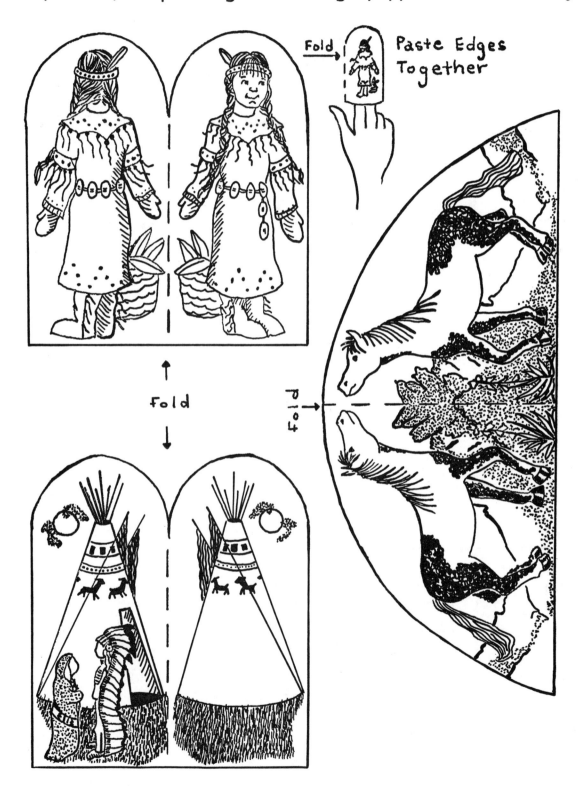

Geometric Shapes/Designs

1. Color and cut out the shapes at the bottom of the page.
2. Arrange the shapes on the blankets below to form the designs shown here.
3. Color the blanket designs shown below with the appropriate colors.

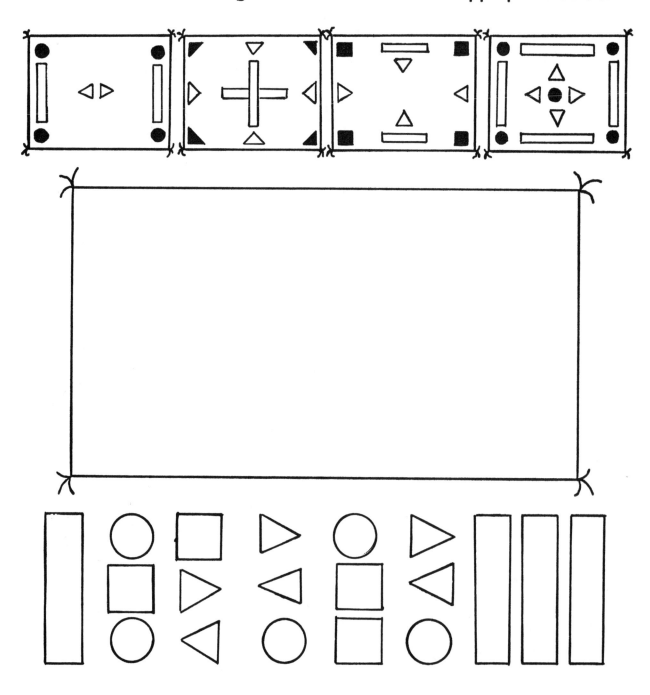

Categorizing Animals Of The Plains

Draw and write the names of some animals of the plains.

Mammals   **Reptiles**   **Birds**

Name _____

Summarizing

Think of short sentences that tell what happened in the story. Write them along the body of the snake. Color the snake. Cut it out and read your summary.

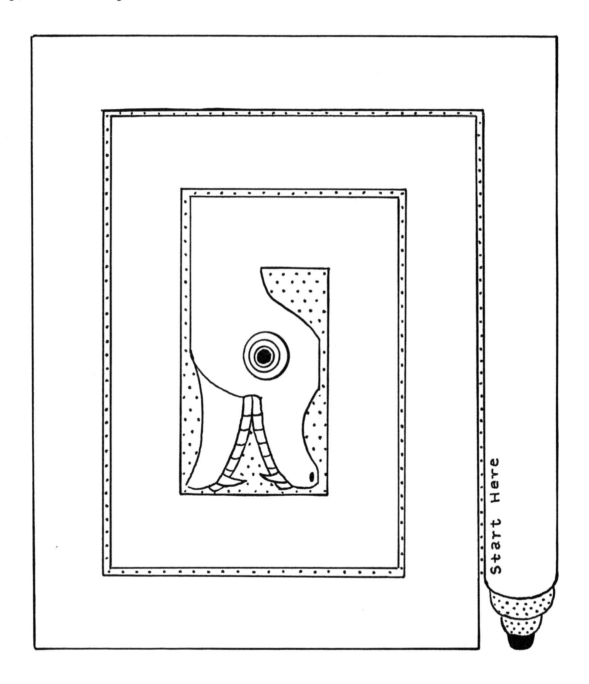

Name _____

Cherokee History

A palisade is a tall fence made of wood. The Cherokee Indians lived in villages with palisades around them. Their houses were made of grass and mud.

Draw a
Cherokee
village with a
palisade

The Cherokee people were happy with their way of life. Then soldiers moved them to another home far away. Their long walk was called "The Trail of Tears."

Draw a picture
to show how
you would feel
if you had to
move from
your home.

A Cherokee man named Sequoyah invented Cherokee writing. Can you copy this?

Name _____

Story Frame

1. In the spaces given below, describe the main character, the problem, and the solution.
2. Illustrate the faces to go with your descriptions.

Main Character:

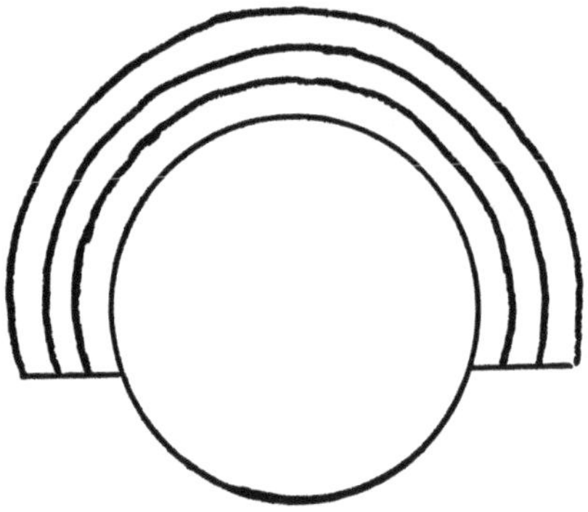

_____

_____

_____

_____

Problem:

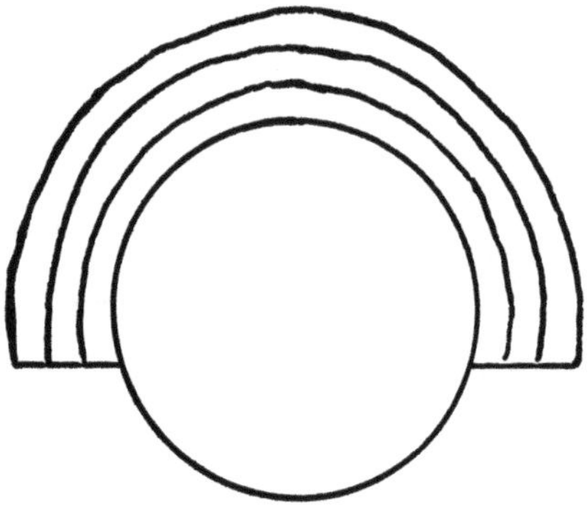

_____

_____

_____

_____

Solution:

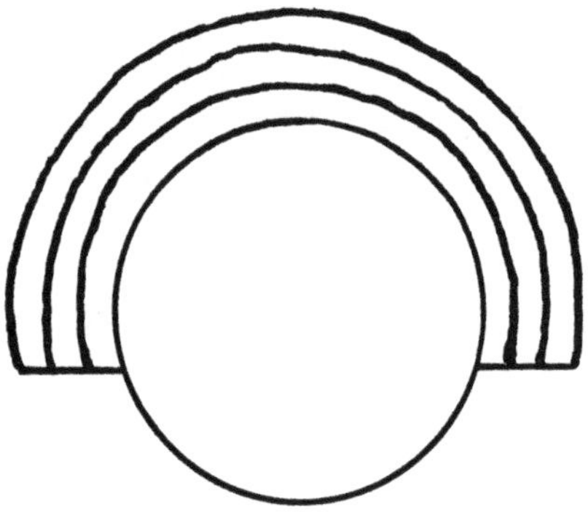

_____

_____

_____

_____

Name _____

66

Patterning

1. Complete the patterns of Rough-Face Girl's necklaces.

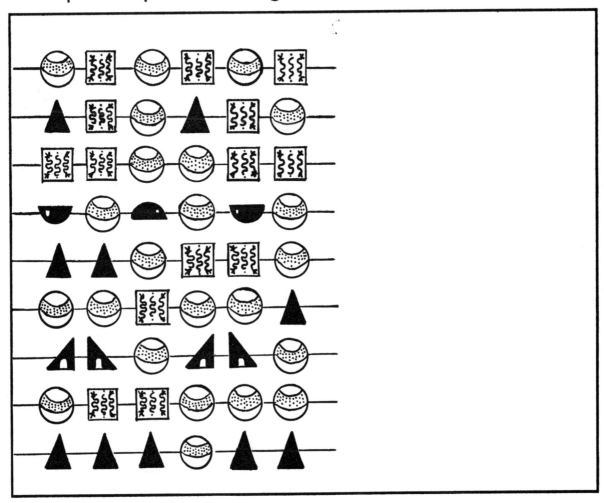

2. Make your own necklace patterns in the space below.

Name _____

Uses For Birch Bark

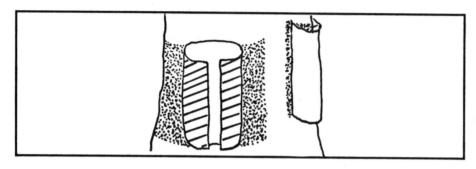

Birch trees have a white bark that peels off easily.

Algonquin Indians used birch bark for many things.

Wigwams were sometimes covered with birch bark.

Draw what is inside this wigwam.

A <u>mocock</u> is a birch bark basket. The bark was cut with designs. Put your design on this one.

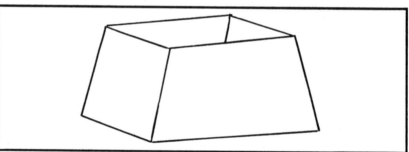

Canoes were made of pieces of birch bark sewn together. The seams were sealed with pine gum. Decorate this canoe.

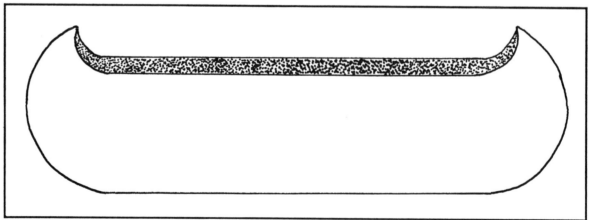

Name _____

Fold Book

Cut out the fold book. Draw pictures and write descriptions of the beginning, middle, and end of the story.

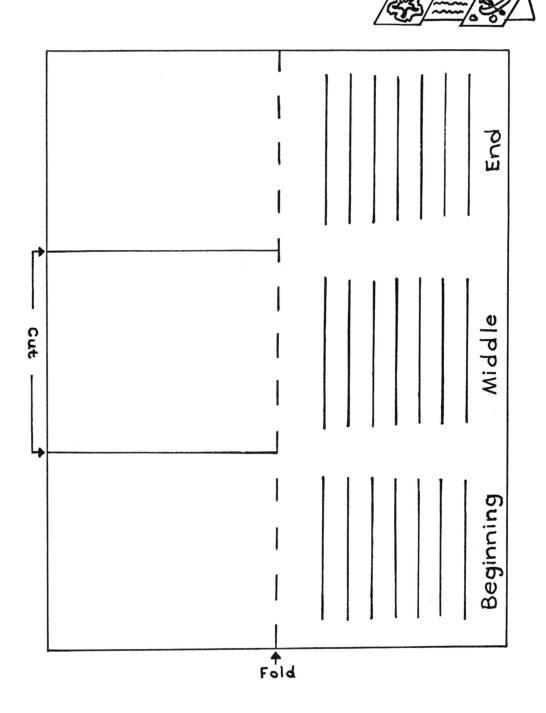

Moccasin Measuring

Trace around your foot in the box at the bottom of this page. Cut it out and decorate it to look like a moccasin. Use it to measure these things:

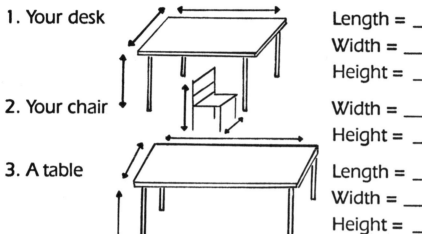

1. Your desk

Length = _____ moccasins
Width = _____ moccasins
Height = _____ moccasins

2. Your chair

Width = _____ moccasins
Height = _____ moccasins

3. A table

Length = _____ moccasins
Width = _____ moccasins
Height = _____ moccasins

4. Draw and write the names of other things you have measured.

_____moccasins   _____moccasins   _____moccasins   _____moccasins

Trace around your foot in this box.

Name _____

Parts Of A Flower

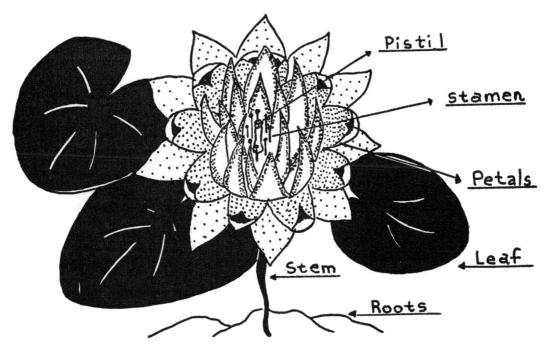

Draw your own flower with all the parts. Describe your flower in the space provided below.

_____

_____

_____

Name _____

Compare/Contrast The First Thanksgiving

Draw a picture of the first
Thanksgiving.

Draw a picture of your
Thanksgiving now.

Draw and describe how the first Thanksgiving was the same as yours.

_____

_____

_____

_____

_____

_____

Draw and describe how the first Thanksgiving was different from yours.

_____

_____

_____

_____

_____

_____

Name _____

Following Directions

Follow the directions to make one of Raven's boxes.

Name _____

Thunderbird Mask

name _____

cut here
headband

cut here
headband

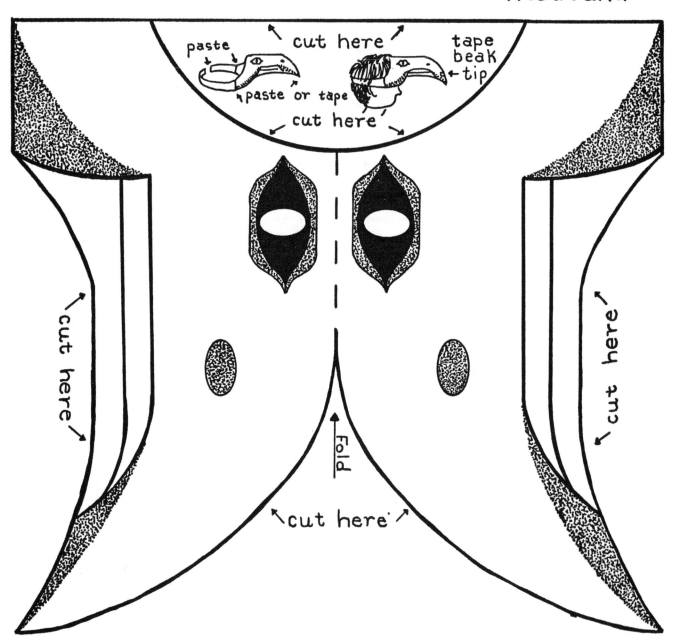

paste

cut here

tape
beak
tip

paste or tape

cut here

cut here

cut here

Fold

cut here

Name _____

Sequencing

Cut out the squares at the
bottom of the page. Paste them
in the correct sequence. Draw a
picture to go with each one.

Draw picture here.   Paste words here.

1

2

3

| Sedna's father threw her into the water because he was afraid. Sedna became goddess of the sea. | Sedna left her home with Mattak. They paddled far across the sea. | Sedna's father came to get her. She went with him because she knew Mattak was a bird-spirit. |

Name _____

Understanding Temperature

Activity #1

Read the temperature on the thermometer. Write it down. Circle the word that tells whether it is hot, warm, cool, cold, or freezing.

   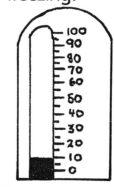

Temp. = _____°F   Temp. = _____°F   Temp. = _____°F   Temp. = _____°F

hot   warm   hot   warm   hot   warm   hot   warm
cool   cold   cool   cold   cool   cold   cool   cold
freezing   freezing   freezing   freezing

Activity #2

Draw in the correct temperature. Then draw and describe what you would wear in that temperature.

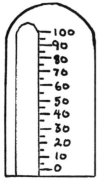   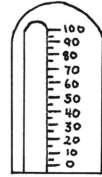

Temp. = 75°F   Temp. = 90°F   Temp. = 5°F   Temp. = 40°F

I wear   I wear   I wear   I wear

_____   _____   _____   _____

Name _____

Arctic Sea Animals

Color each animal.
Paint over the finished picture with blue watercolor.

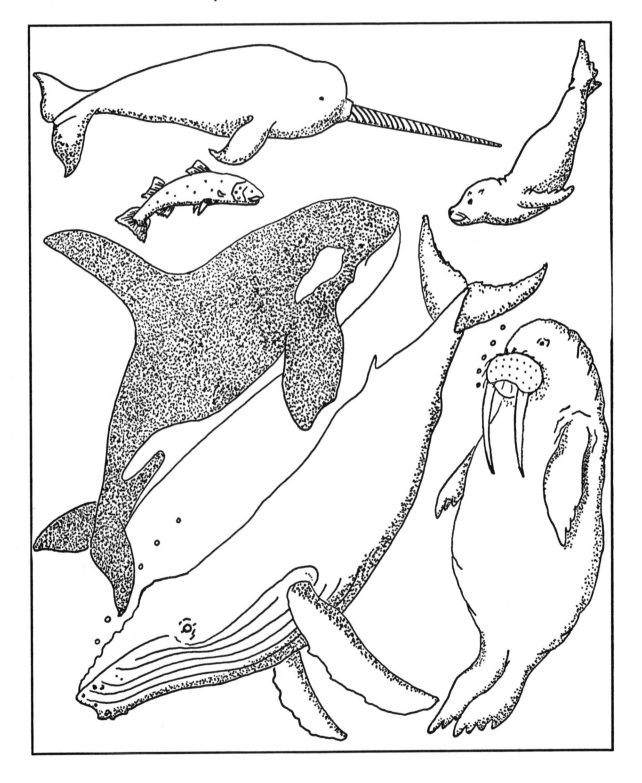

Name _____

MORE ACTIVITIES FOR NATIVE AMERICAN STUDY

Diary of a Day
Write and draw an account of what a day would be like for a child of a particular Indian tribe.

Life-Size Model
Construct a life-size model of an Indian home:
- Tepee (Plains)
- Longhouse (Northwest)
- Village w/palisade (Cherokee)
- Hogan (Southwest)
- Wigwam (Algonquin)
- Igloo (Eskimo)

Plant Native American Crops
Plant corn, beans, pumpkin, and sunflower seeds. Cultivate them and monitor their growth.

Weaving Boards
Cut a piece of cardboard to form an 8" x 10" weaving board. Notch the top and bottom, and string with yarn. Weave yarn back and forth.

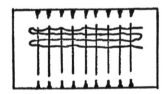

Re-create the First Thanksgiving
Dress up like Pilgrims and authentic Algonquin Indians to re-create the first Thanksgiving. Share this experience with another class. Let one class be the Pilgrims and the other be the Indians; then teach each other what you've learned.

Soapcarving
The Eskimos carved ivory to create Arctic animals. Use soap to fashion Arctic animals.

Out of the Mouths of Chiefs
Read aloud the famous words of such great chiefs as Chief Joseph, Black Elk, and Red Cloud. Discuss their meaning in modern terms. Discuss their dilemmas.

Mural
Have the class make a mural of the Native American regions studied in this unit.

Pottery
Obtain ceramic clay and let the children make coil pots like those of the Southwest Indians. Have the pots fired in a kiln.

Native American Games
Learn to play Native American games, such as Lacrosse, Leap Frog, and Cat's Cradle.

Grind Corn
Use a mortar and pestle to grind corn into cornmeal. Use the cornmeal to make tortillas for the class to eat.

Collections/Speakers
Invite community people who have collections of Indian arrowheads, baskets, etc., to visit the class. Ask them to show their artifacts and share their knowledge of specific tribes.

More Native Americans
There are many other regional Native Americans that deserve study. California Indians, Indians of the Great Basin, those of the Sub-Arctic, the Mound Builders of the Mississippi and Ohio Valleys, the Seminole of Florida, and the ancient Anasazi of the Southwest are a few of these.

Bibliography

Brother Eagle, Sister Sky, by Susan Jeffers. New York: Dial Books, 1991.

Dancing Drum, by Terri Cohlene. New Jersey: Watermill Press, 1990.

The Girl Who Loved Wild Horses, by Paul Goble. New York: Aladdin Books, 1978.

How Raven Brought Light To People, by Ann Dixon. New York: Margaret K. McElderry Books, 1992.

The Legend of the Bluebonnet, by Tomie dePaola. New York: G.P. Putnam's Sons, 1983.

The Rough-Face Girl, by Rafe Martin. New York: G.P. Putnam's Sons, 1992.

Song of Sedna, by Robert D. San Souci. New York: Doubleday, 1981.

The Star Maiden, by Barbara Juster Esbensen. New York: Little, Brown & Company, 1988.

Turquoise Boy, by Terri Cohlene. New Jersey: Watermill Press, 1990.

When Clay Sings, by Byrd Baylor. New York: Aladdin Books, 1972.

For Further Study of Native Americans

Native Americans

Ancient America, by Marion Wood. New York: Facts on File, 1990.

Children of the Earth and Sky, by Stephen Krensky. New York: Scholastic Press, 1991.

Pictorial History of the North American Indian, by Bill Yenne and Susan Garratt. New York: Exeter Books, 1984.

Plains

Iktomi and the Buffalo Skull, by Paul Goble.* New York: Orchard Books, 1991.

Quillworker, by Terri Cohlene. New Jersey: Watermill Press, 1990.

Where the Buffaloes Begin, by Olaf Baker. New York: Puffin Books, 1981.

Southwest

The Anasazi, by David Petersen. Chicago: Children's Press, 1991.

Annie and the Old One, by Miska Miles. Boston: Little, Brown & Company, 1971.

The Desert is Theirs, by Byrd Baylor.** New York: Aladdin Books, 1975.

Knots of a Counting Rope, Bill Martin, Jr. and John Archambault. New York: Henry Holt and Company, 1987.

Algonquin

Dream Catcher, by Audrey Osofsky. New York: Orchard Books, 1992.

Little Firefly, by Terri Cohlene. New Jersey: Watermill Press, 1990.

Northwest

Clamshell Boy, by Terri Cohlene. New Jersey: Watermill Press, 1990.

The Enchanted Caribou, by Elizabeth Cleaver. New York: Atheneum, 1985.

Raven's Light, by Susan Hand Shetterly. New York: Atheneum, 1991.

Eskimo

Arctic Memories, by Normee Ekoomiak. New York: Henry Holt and Company, 1988.

Ka-Ha-Si and the Loon, by Terri Cohlene. New Jersey: Watermill Press, 1990.

*   Paul Goble's books are excellent for the study of Plains Indians.
**   Byrd Baylor has other books about native people and animals of the Southwest desert.